■ SCHOLASTIC

News

Nonfiction Readers®

What Is Air Force One?

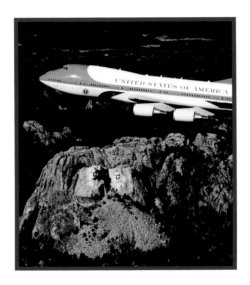

By Amanda Miller

Children's Press®
An Imprint of Scholastic Inc.
New York Toronto London Auckland Sydney
Mexico City New Delhi Hong Kong
Danbury, Connecticut

These content vocabulary word builders are for grades 1–2.

Subject Consultant: Eli J. Lesser, MA, Director of Education, National Constitution Center, Philadelphia, Pennsylvania

Reading Consultant: Cecilia Minden-Cupp, PhD, Early Literacy Consultant and Author, Chapel Hill, North Carolina

Photographs © 2009: Corbis Images: 19, 23 bottom left (Bettmann), 4 bottom left, 10 (Bob Daemmrich), 23 top left (Chris Greenberg/CNP), back cover, 9 (Brooks Kraft), 5 bottom right, 8 (William Manning/www.williammanning.com), 5 bottom left, 6 (Martin H. Simon), cover (George Tiedemann/GT Images); Department of Defense: 2, 5 top left, 18 left (TSGT Mike Buytas, USAF); George Bush Presidential Library and Museum: 11 bottom; Michael Davis Photography: 7 top, 20, 21; NEWSCOM: 4 top, 5 top right, 14, 18 right (Olivier Douliery/ABACA), 15 top, 23 top right (Paul J. Richards/ AFP), 11 top (Zuma Press); Redux Pictures/Stephen Crowley/The New York Times: 13; Reuters/Mark Wilson: 17; Courtesy of the Ronald Reagan Presidential Library: 4 bottom right, 12, 15 bottom, 23 bottom right; U.S. Air Force: 1, 7 bottom.

Series Design: Simonsays Design!
Art Direction, Production, and Digital Imaging: Scholastic Classroom Magazines

Library of Congress Cataloging-in-Publication Data

Miller, Amanda, 1974-
What Is Air Force One? / Amanda Miller.
   p. cm. - (Scholastic news nonfiction readers)

Includes bibliographical references and index.
ISBN 13: 978-0-531-21089-5 (lib. bdg.)   978-0-531-22426-7 (pbk.)
ISBN 10: 0-531-21089-8 (lib. bdg.)   0-531-22426-0 (pbk.)
1. Air Force One (Presidential aircraft)–Juvenile literature. 2. Presidents–Transportation–United States–Juvenile literature. I. Title.
TL723.M55 2008
387.7'42088352230973–dc22   2008029602

6 7 8 9 10 R 18 17 16 15 14 13

CONTENTS

WORD HUNT

Look for these words as you read. They will be in **bold**.

guard
(gard)

office
(**off**-iss)

pilots
(**pye**-luhts)

hangar
(**hang**-ur)

menu
(**men**-yoo)

plane
(plane)

White House
(wite houss)

What Is Air Force One?

Air Force One is the President's **plane**. It's not like any other plane. It has everything the President needs to do a big job!

plane

Air Force One has the words "United States of America" on its side.

The President lives and works in the **White House** most of the time.

When he travels, the President lives and works on Air Force One. Some people call it The Flying White House.

White House

Air Force One is taller than a five-story building.

There is an **office** on the plane. It is a quiet place for the President to do work.

People who work with the President also fly on Air Force One. They may talk around a table.

office

President Carter talks on the phone.

President George H.W. Bush holds a meeting.

There is a bedroom on the plane. It has two beds. The President can rest here on long trips.

The **pilots** don't rest! The pilots stay awake and fly the plane.

pilots

President George W. Bush rests on a long trip.

Air Force One has a kitchen. The President's favorite meals are on the **menu**! The President chooses what he wants to eat. Then a chef cooks the meals.

menu

There is always something good to eat, like brownies, on Air Force One!

The President's family can ride on the plane too. Sometimes the President even takes the family pet along!

If you flew on Air Force One, who would come along with you?

President Clinton took his family and his dog, Buddy, on Air Force One.

Air Force One is kept in a **hangar** when it is not flying. A **guard** watches it all day and night. Workers keep it clean. Air Force One is always ready to fly at any moment!

hangar

guard

THE PRESIDENT'S AIRPLANE

"Air Force One" is radio code for the plane that carries the President. He often flies in a Boeing 747 like this one.

The cockpit, where the pilots sit

The presidential seal

A galley, or kitchen

UNITED STATES OF A

The President's rooms: office, dining room, bedroom, bathroom, and shower

The medical room, with medical supplies and an operating table

The jet engines can make the plane fly more than 600 miles per hour.

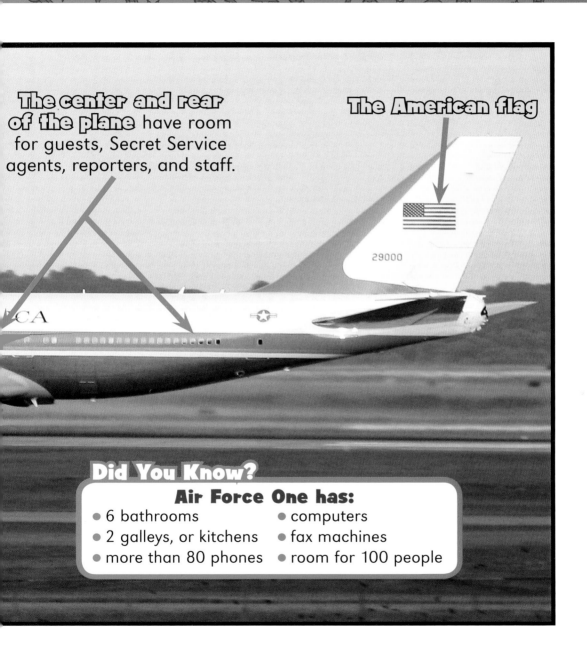

The center and rear of the plane have room for guests, Secret Service agents, reporters, and staff.

The American flag

29000

Did You Know?

Air Force One has:
- 6 bathrooms
- 2 galleys, or kitchens
- more than 80 phones
- computers
- fax machines
- room for 100 people

YOUR NEW WORDS

guard (gard) someone who keeps watch over a place

hangar (**hang**-ur) a big building in which airplanes are kept

menu (**men**-yoo) a list of foods to choose from

office (**off**-iss) a room where someone can work

pilots (**pye**-luhts) people who fly airplanes

plane (plane) a machine with wings that flies through the air

White House (wite houss) the home and office of the United States President

ON THE JOB
ON AIR FORCE ONE

**President
George W. Bush**

**President
Bill Clinton**

**President
Jimmy Carter**

**President
Ronald Reagan**

INDEX

FIND OUT MORE

Book:

January, Brendan. *Air Force One*. New York: Scholastic, 2004.

Website:

http://people.howstuffworks.com/air-force-one.htm

MEET THE AUTHOR

Amanda Miller is a writer and editor for Scholastic. She and her dog, Henry, live in Brooklyn, New York.